THE HIPPIE HANDBOOK

A GUIDE FOR TURNING ON TUNING IN AND DROPPING OUT

INTRODUCTION

HI there – my name is Stuart Hampton and I am someone who has always been drawn to hippie lifestyle – Hippie culture – Cosmic considerations and the exploration of time, space and reality. This book is based on feelings and opinions I have which come from my heart – im not trying to preach or to judge, its all just feelings I have about things. These feelings all started to really begin to take shape when I reached the age of about 15 and I started to be drawn to the 'vibrations' from the golden egg that is the 'hippie' culture. I started listening to the Beatles – I smoked a lot of pot, I started meditating and doing yoga, and I started to learn to play the guitar and became a vegetarian. I then went to university and did a degree in psychology and eventually met a load of hippies who shared my perspective in life and slowly things started to fall in to place. I started exploring who I was by wearing colorful clothes and being more certain about who's team I was on in this world – I decided that 'Peace & Love' was where it was at and that for the rest of my life I would be committed to this cause as to my heart and my innermost self it was all that made any sense, it was the only sane aspiration to have as far as I could see.

It can be hard to find one's way in this world and you really just have to follow your heart but for me the hippie vibration really gave me some good signposts and a sense of direction and purpose. My intuition eventually lead me to follow my spiritual calling for enlightenment so that I might begin to understand the cosmic secrets of consciousness and the universe which to this day I am still doing. I went to live in a spiritual retreat center for 4 and a half years where I studied many esoteric and new age traditions in spirituality such as shamanism, yoga, meditation, zen, sound healing and much more.

So what is 'Hippie' – what does it mean to be a hippie and what are the ideals within the hippie philosophy?

In my humble opinion, being a hippie is all about following the deep desire to **HARMONISE** – To become **IN-TUNE** with the self, the earth and the universe. To live **PEACEFULLY** and with **LOVE**. To learn to **CO-OPERATE** in a state of **SYMBIOSIS** – and live in a way which is **TRUE** – **ENERGISED** – **OPEN** and **REAL**.

HONESTY and the **LOVING OPEN EMBRACE** of **NATURE** and of **LIFE** is important to the hippie movement. It is also about **CREATIVITY** – **EXPRESSION** and **JOY**.

I believe that the hippie movement is one of the nicest cultures and sets of ideals that we have ever created – I believe that there is a hippy in the heart of all of us, and really, peace and love is all we really want and need. Peace and love is healthy for life, healthy for the planet and brings calm and happiness to the mind. The hippie way as far as I see it has been approved by the universe as the quintessential way to live as everything thrives when there is love and peace.

I believe that the Hippie aspiration comes from a much deeper place, and a part of us that we all need to nourish. I believe that this need to harmonise comes from the need to seek union and oneness. To align perfectly and melt into the sea of infinite consciousness. I believe that this is our true calling in life and our true destination, however long it may take for us to reach 'Nirvana' I believe that it is the fundamental aspiration of the heart and soul and through our pain and our joy we navigate through the sea of consciousness until we are at one with 'The Almighty' – whatever this might be for you, God, The true self, Gaia, Jah, Universal energy.

In peace we find love and in love we find peace.

TAKING STEPS TOWARDS HARMONY

So, if the hippie vibe is all about harmonising the self how does one go about taking steps to move towards a place of harmony?

Well, I can tell you a few things that have helped me along the way. First comes the 'Intention' – The deep sense in the heart that what you want, need and desire is to find peace, That for you peace and truth and understanding is more important then being rich, famous and powerful. That your goal is like an opening to the universe, a humble wish to 'know'. This deep wish is something very personal, that is like a contract between you and the universe – it is a vibration in your heart that has nothing to do with anything you can 'do' physically. It is a deep commitment in the mind that cannot be expressed in words or actions. It is not something that is going to make you 'better' then other people, or something thats gonna give you power, it is very subtle, very pure and rooted in truth.

From this seed of intention beautiful things can begin to grow and you will find it will guide you, like a magnet – towards things that bring you more and more peace. Once the intention has been established one then begins to look at ones actions and deeds in the world and starts to try and understand how actions create consequences and we begin to see what kind of person and influence we want to be in this life.

HIPPY MUSIC

One of the first major helpful steps towards developing a hippie state of consciousness is to explore the ocean of music that swims around the earth day and night. I first began to realise I was a hippy when I became interested in the psychedelic music from the 60's and 70's and that to me the Woodstock music festival was a true vision of heaven. I started learning to play the guitar at around the age of 16 and was listening to a lot of well known hippie groovers like Jimi Hendrix, The Beatles, The Doors, Pink Floyd, Crosby Stills and Nash, Joni Mitchel and Kate Bush to name but a few. I feel that learning an instrument is a great way to unlock the soul and give you another way to express the in-expressable. When I learned to play the guitar it was like a personal revolution in the development of my consciousness. I felt as though I had been given a new voice and it was such a relief to find a channel through which to express these deep swirly thoughts and feelings.

If you have any kind of confidence issues just start small and work your way up. I had many and I found that just by taking slow and manageable steps one can learn to open up more and more. I first started by singing in the shower, knowing that people outside could hear me – it was like a way to first begin to sing in public. I eventually learned to sing and perform on stage and now I don't think there would be any confidence issues for me and I could probably perform in front of the whole world if I had to. I feel that learning to sing, play an instrument and perform in public is a great spiritual lesson in life that can help you learn to let go, to 'go with the flow' and trust in yourself. It also teaches you telepathic connection and deep listening and sensitivity towards 'vibes' – especially when you start to play with other people. I feel that music has the capacity to summon up magic and transform the energy and the atmosphere and in turn elevate consciousness. When one learns to use these energies and change the 'vibes' its almost like practicing magic, you become like a wizard, casting your magic spells of peace and love.

Learning to play and perform has also been a godsend for me because it has helped me to make friends with people and connect to places and to people. When I moved to a new town once in Wales, I didn't know anyone and had no connections to the place, no job and no real reason to be there. Luckily I could play the guitar so I went to all the open mike nights at the bars around town and performed a lot, I also started my own open mike night and soon got to know a lot of people and became quite connected to the town. I actually find performing and singing easier then socialising, in many ways i'm quite introverted, but its strange, once you find your groove with music and performing it can soon become easier and more comfortable as a social transaction then just having a conversation. Its like something that can heal you, and something that can comfort you and that you can fall back on.

I love singing songs that everyone can join in with – its so lovely when everyone is singing together, I feel like it can transport us to this place of cosmic union – and for a moment we can experience that sweet sense of togetherness, of oneness.

If your busy being a hippy too and you find yourself out of work because you've been spending too much time daydreaming and surfing the waves of cosmic consciousness playing music can be a great way to earn a few extra magic beans to spend. Iv done lots of busking (playing music in the streets for passers by to throw you a few magic beans) its really fun, and I feel that its a great service to society bringing music and good vibes to the streets. Its a great way to connect with your local town and you are likely to meet some lovely people. I also did door to door busking when I lived in Cornwall in England – where basically I dressed up in a purple suit and top-hat and went door to door offering to play a song in exchange for 1 pound. At the time I was raising money to go to India, which I successfully managed to do, I got arrested twice (turns out you need a license to go door to door) but it was quite an adventure.

I really feel that bringing music to the people is such a wonderful gift. When I was doing door to door busking I had a few encounters that were super lovely – one of them was with an old woman who lived on her own, you could tell that she rarely had any visitors and the air in the house felt quite colourless, she was probably quite lonely – I went into her house and chatted with her for a while, had a cup of tea then I played her the song 'everybody's talking' by Neilson – she absolutely loved it, and got quite emotional, she stood up, held out her arms and said a prayer for me, and then gave me a bible. It was so sweet. So, if you learn to access your musical energies and find ways of transmitting peace and love through music, share it with people who need it the most, send them your love and show them your freedom. The more free you are, truly free, the more you liberate others. Music is a great way to open hearts and minds, your own, and other peoples.

Music can also be a very spiritual practice and during my time in the commune I became familiar with various forms of Bhakti Yoga – which is the art-form of practicing the union of the self with the divine through singing. The word 'Yoga' means union and is often referring to the cosmic union of the self with 'god'.

Chanting can be used as a meditational tool and a way of communicating with the divine cosmic angels. You can send your deepest prayers and sentiments to the ether on the waves of a chant. It can also help to heal your sadness and strengthen the soul. I have chanted a few times in my life when I have felt lost and a bit weak in my soul.

One of my favorite chants is -

'Om Mani Padme Hum'

I particularly like this chant because I once saw a three year old girl go in to a deep trance and start chanting this chant. She was one of the most amazing little girls I have ever encountered. It was when I was living in the spiritual retreat/hippie commune. We often had courses and teachers come to our center and there was one I used to do every year – it was Don Conreaux's Gongmaster training course. It was a 10-day retreat where you would learn to master the art of sound healing using gongs, singing bowls and other instruments. It was a very very cosmic course that involved lots of far out rituals and practices including blind folded trance dancing, all-night gong puja meditations and more – and by the end of the 10 days it was common for everyone to literally be on another planet, in another dimension – totally elevated in consciousness and wide open. Well, during one year, there was a single mother on the course and she brought her daughter with her, an amazing, angelic, fairy-like cosmic princess from the divine world – who reminded me of the purity of the human heart and the innocence and the love that we have from birth that can sometimes get lost or distorted. Well, this girl was like a doorway into the angelic realms, her face was the face of an angel – and she understood completely what was important – vibes, peace and love was her only concern and she seemed to have a telepathic link with people, often expressing things that they were thinking, she did that with me on numerous occasions. Anyway, this little girl attended the whole retreat with us, and everyone fell completely in love with her – at the end of the retreat we were all sat around the campfire in the evening – and we were singing, in union, I was playing my guitar and the little girl was playing. She then became more and more excited and started asking me to sing her name, so we all started to sing her name – she then rolled her eyes, sat on a log, closed her eyes and suddenly became so still, like a puppet on strings. Her movements were perfect and precise, completely unlike those of a three year old girls movements – she raised her arms up to her heart, did an opening motion, lifted her arms up to the sky then put them in prayer position and started bowing – and then she started chanting 'Om mani padme hum' – and she did this for about 10 minutes. At the same time, we all fell completely silent, the atmosphere was charged and energized and we all felt waves of bliss and cosmic energy surging up our spines – it was absolutely amazing, like I had just witnessed a miracle. It was impossible for me to be skeptical because it was a three year old girl, and I saw it right before my eyes – for me it was evidence that there is a cosmic consciousness and that there is an ethereal realm that we can commune with. Even the most skeptical of the group was astonished by what happened. For me it also helped to confirm the validity of this particular chant.

The chant 'Om Mani Padme Hum' originated from Tibet and is a call to the green goddess Tara who resides in the heart. It is an attempt to awaken the jewel of compassion which resides in the heart of every being. Try it for yourself – I have been told that the correct pronunciation of this chant is -

'OM Mani Payme Hung'

But it is written '**Om Mani Padme Hum**'

Give it a go for yourself and see if it helps to awaken the sweet jewel of compassion inside your tender heart.

Another great sound to make when chanting is 'Om' sometimes wrote as '**Aum**' ॐ – this is thought to be the sound of the universe and I believe that this sound carries a very healing vibration. In Hinduism 'Aum' is often wrote as a symbol, that little squiggle that looks a bit like a 3 and a 0 joined together. Sit on the floor in a meditation position making sure that your diaphragm and chest area has plenty of room to breathe easy, and with full and relaxed breathing make the sound of 'Aum' going through each syllable from open to closed mouth.

When I lived in the hippie commune we also used to sing a number of lovely shamanistic songs that have been used for generations around campfires by native American Indians and groovy hippies – here are a couple of my favorites -

Mother I feel you under my feet
Mother I feel your heart beat
Hey ya Hey ya Hey ya Hey ya Hey ya Hey ho
Hey ya Hey ya Hey ya Hey ya Hey ya Hey ho

And another....

The river is flowing, flowing and flowing, the river is flowing back to the sea
Mother Earth carry me, your child I will always be, Mother Earth carry me, back to the sea

Ohh, and I just remembered another....

Tall trees, warm fire, strong wind, cool water
I feel you in my body, and I feel you in the source

They are a bit like chants, you sing them over and over around a campfire, maybe with some drums and percussion – they help to encourage a sense of group connectivity and summon up the great spirit. They can also help to induce a trance like state that can help you synchronize with the rhythms of the universal dance of life.

Chants and sound vibrations are very important for health and well-being. A study by Japanese scientist Dr Masuro Emoto on the effects of sound vibration on the development of water crystals shown without doubt that thoughts, sounds, consciousness and intentions are all linked in a profound and subtle way. 'Positive' thoughts, sounds and intentions such as classical music, prayers and words like 'peace' when directed at a glass of water caused beautiful symmetrical elaborate water crystals to be formed when the water was frozen and observed under a microscope. Conversely, when so called 'negative' stimuli was exposed to the water, distorted, warped a-symmetrical water crystals were produced. This in my opinion is one of the most important scientific discoveries of our age as it helps to reveal the dynamics of this universe and how there is almost a natural language that is built in to the very fabric of our world that is based on vibrations, consciousness and mandala's. Check it our for your self, there are some very good video's online on sites such as Youtube about it, and he has also written a beautiful book about his study that i'd recommend.

GREAT HIPPIE MUSIC TO LISTEN TO...

Captain Beefheart
Crosby, Stills and Nash
Blind Faith
Joni Mitchel
Jimi Hendrix
Joe Cocker
Strawberry Alarm Clock Band
Jefferson Airplane
Captain Beyond
The Who
The Rolling Stones
Bonzo Dog Doo Dah Band
Curtis Mayfield
Kula Shaker
David Bowie
Kate Bush
Ravi Shankar
John Lennon
Simon & Garfunkel
Fairport Convention
King Crimson
Pond
Orange Alabaster Mushroom
Love
Groundhogs

Richie Havens
The Doors
The Beatles
Pink Floyd
Canned Heat
Jethro Tull
Caravan
Ultimate Spinach
Camel
Led Zeppelin
Santana
Melanie
Sly and the Family Stone
Roxy Music
Janis Joplin
Supertramp
George Harrison
Genesis
Donovan
Wings
Yes
Krishna Das
Ravi Shankar
Cream
Curtis Mayfield

Hare Kṛṣṇa
Hare Kṛṣṇa
Kṛṣṇa Kṛṣṇa
Hare Hare
Hare Rāma
Hare Rāma
Rāma Rāma
Hare Hare

GROOVY CLOTHES

It seems to go hand in hand throughout the ages that hippies have been known to have a very groovy and psychedelic fashion sense, so yeah, to be a full-blown hippie it can be a good idea to experiment with how you dress. It can feel real nice to push the borders and break down social norms by wearing outrageous and groovy outfits. When I was at university I began to find myself, I became more free about expressing love, learned to play the guitar and sing in public and then, became more free and experimental about my fashion sense, wearing things like purple suits, top-hats and bright yellow psychedelic sunglasses. To be honest it felt fantastic to express myself. It was like a huge out-breath. Like all my life I had been breathing in, and in, and in – swallowing what people had told me (to some extent) and wearing clothes that I felt didn't really reflect the person I was on the inside. Relaxing about clothes and fashion and just being playful is a great way to begin to 'find yourself' and experiment with your sense of identity.

Often hippies wear brightly colored clothes, Indian garments, African garments and retro flower power clothes from the 60's and 70's. They might tie a bandanna in their hair and wear cool accessories like prayer beads, 'om' necklaces and so on. I think its lovely, like the hippie uniform. Its like saying 'this is the team that I am on' – 'I am one of these hippie people' – a seeker of mind expansion, consciousness and love – a harmonizer and a pilgrim for peace.

In society we are all under a spell of 'normal' – we go around trying to maintain the 'normal' and keep things functioning on a level that we all feel makes sense. We like to be able to look at people and think 'ah, they are like this, or that and so on and so forth...' we like to make judgments about what people are and like a pantomime society plays out and we all play our part. Hippies traditionally are the non-conformists – the people who try and 'think outside the box' and do things differently. They pride themselves on freedom of speech and freedom of action and answer to a higher source beyond governments. They answer to mother nature and the universal laws which govern our hearts. Playing the part of the hippie in society is a beautiful and noble cause and part of a social movement that has been unfolding for a long time.

Hippies have been known to get involved in political action, protests and wear symbols from various social justice movements on their outfits. One such symbol is the traditional CND peace sign which originated from 'campaign for nuclear disarmament' – an anti-war movement who protest against war and the war machine which profits from the sale of bombs and arms which cause mass destruction and devastation. You can incorporate these symbols into your clothes if you find any groups that you might feel reflect your heart-felt needs for peace and fairness. A few other groups worth mentioning that you might wish to check out include the ALF (animal liberation front) – Greenpeace – Sea Shepherd – Campaign against the arms trade – Animal Aid – AMMA foundation – to name but a few.

So, wearing groovy clothes is much more then just looking good, it is linking yourself to an on-going wave of like-minded souls who feel inspired to try and promote the core hippie values of peace love and understanding. Eventually, depending on which path you take – the need to make change will probably begin to fall away – and you will find peace – but the nice thing is, you will probably still be a hippie, you may still wear the hippie uniform and wear the symbols and maybe take part in the marches – but hopefully, you will have found peace inside yourself and will feel liberated from the physical world. I love hippie fashion as I feel that it helps recruit more seekers in the world and helps to add a bit of colour and groovy-ness to our world. Shine on you crazy diamond.

FREE LOVE

In this human life we all crave 'freedom'. We seek to express ourselves and be in the 'flow' and crave the ability to get what we want whenever we want it. It annoys us when things don't go the way we want them to or we can sometimes feel restricted by others and controlled. Sometimes the presence of other people makes us feel inhibited and there is a little ball of energy in the pit of our stomachs that feels like it just wants to jump, shout, express itself, be heard and break free from the chains of social norms and values. Free from the suffocating grip of logic and sense and social protocol. Sometimes we don't want to be polite, say please and thank-you and smile all the time. Sometimes we feel like jumping up and down, taking our clothes off, taking someone elses' clothes off and just being 'free'.

In modern day life we have to deal with and manage so many powerful and strange energies and instincts. We feel that we have to be civilized and intelligent and respond appropriately in social situations so that we don't cause offense and so we can maintain our status within our pier group. Its like we have to wear a mask and maintain a persona that we use to project ourselves in the world but underneath that mask there is sometimes a crazy, illogical, playful, lustful, sexual, creative and expressive being also. For years I have struggled with this urge to be free and still do.

For many of us we are trying to discover our 'real' selves and try to live in alignment with this 'true' self. This can manifest in so many ways, one of the main ways is through our sense of identity. We choose various things in the world and ways of being that we feel represent who we are. We might wear certain clothes, say certain words, listen to certain music and dream certain dreams all because we feel that this represents who we are. Indeed we often talk about people in this way, we say 'oh, that's not like her' or 'that is just like her' – how do we know? What does it mean to be 'like' anything? We are all so complex and multi-layered how do we end up falling in to these boxes of definition?
Often in my life iv felt restriction by my box of definition, by my hippie image and mannerisms, from being that person who is all about peace and love, and from other peoples perceptions of me. People remember who I am and what I am like and every time I see them they expect me to behave in the same ways that they have become accustomed to. This can sometimes feel restrictive and limit a sense of possibility and freedom.

For a long time I felt that I wasn't able to be as affectionate and loving as I wanted to be. I wanted to touch people more, to hug them, kiss them sometimes and often I would find myself falling in love with people. Often because of social norms and values and my uncertainty about whether or not I was 'allowed' to express my affection or if they would be receptive to it I would deny these urges and just stuff them down and lock them away inside Pandora's box somewhere deep inside my psyche.

As I got older and after spending time in the hippie commune and exploring who I was and this sense of being authentic and being 'free' I started to push the boundaries of my sense of self definition and perhaps do things that I wouldn't do normally or do different things in various social situations such as stop smiling as much if I didn't feel like smiling (i'd still feel happy inside, I just wouldn't need to move my face to express that). I also at times started to try and conquer fear by hugging people more, being more tactile. When I went out in nightclubs I used to hug strangers and at times this got me in to trouble as sometimes the people I hugged didn't want to be hugged. I also became more liberal about how I felt sexually. I think becoming more relaxed about sex did teach me something, and at times I felt as though I was at one with the universe during my sexual explorations. But from my experiences I feel that integrity with sexual relationships is very important and should always be treated respectfully.

But what is this burning need for 'freedom' that we all feel? I feel that it is something much deeper and more profound then anything we can do in the world. I believe that it relates to the sense the soul has from being trapped inside a material body in a material world and being made to take part in this cosmic expression of form and change. I believe that this soul is limitless, undefined and timeless yet it has been thrust into existence and locked inside a body and a world filled with limits and definitions. This I believe causes a struggle between the real self (i.e. the limitless soul) and the temporary self (i.e. the body and the world). The dynamics between the two are difficult because the limited material world could never adequately express the true greatness of the soul because in its essence it is defined and limited whereas the soul is not limited. So there is always this struggle for identity in the material world, we try and find a way to be who we really are (the limitless soul) but it is impossible to be it in this world, so the struggle is endless.

Freedom I feel can be partly realised when we stop trying to find 'ourselves' in this limited (but very beautiful) material world. We recognise that we are limitless, eternal spirit souls experiencing the expressions of form and limitation that this world is offering us. Like watching a movie, we don't believe that we 'are' the movie when we are watching it – so this kind of detachment, in a relaxed, loving and gentle way, can free us from the endless struggle of 'identity' and need to 'express' who we are inside and we can just enjoy this world for what it is, a beautiful shadow, a cosmic dance, a living profound poem.

It doesn't matter anymore if we cant 'express' ourselves, jump up and down, take our clothes off and sleep with whoever we want to because we are no longer identified with the world. We are able to recognise that we are an unlimited soul that no words or actions could ever adequately describe. So, we are no longer dissatisfied with impermanent ever-changing moments of 'almost' feeling whole, free and complete as we begin to make our way home and find that ever-present immensity of living unlimited consciousness that we are and always have been. The great silence, the is-ness. 'free love' already exists and we are that. Free love needs not to be expressed necessarily, because love is eternally free.

God is love.

Living Magically

This world we live in can be experienced in many different ways and on many different levels. We all walk around experiencing the world subjectively in our own personal self-created and self-sustained reality. The mind maps we create and use to translate the stimuli we receive from the external world make up our perceptions and experiences of reality. To a large extent we can choose how we wish to experience the world we live in. if we cultivate love, openness, magic and focus on divinity, beauty and possibility the world can begin to look extraordinary, like a fairy-tale filled with strange characters, animals, goblins, aliens and fairies. People can begin to look dream-like and magical. Insects can look like strange alien robots from outer-space. Animals begin to look like living cartoon characters, almost like living stuffed toys. The world can then begin to seem like a poem-in-motion. Like a living song, or a magical mandala-like dance that is unfolding like a rose wrapped up in eternity and divinity. I believe reality is much more pliable and fluid then we might assume. And what is considered 'normal' is often 'extraordinary' when one pays a bit more attention and opens up the mind.

In our society we are taught this attitude of 'normalizing' everything so that we just go around thinking everything is OK, and we just 'get on with it'. But what is 'normal' about this life? It is the most extraordinary unfathomable and deeply profound thing ever, even a piece of chewing gum in the street can be seen as a window into the awareness of the ultra-trippy nature of the every day world that we experience. Look closely at things, and open a window in your mind. Instead of making your mind up about the world and deciding that this is this and that is that try and see the world through the eyes of someone who just doesn't know. We are often taught to be afraid of the unknown. We try and box everything up into definitions, words, thoughts and ideas. We use science, philosophy, books and symbols to give us a sense that we know whats going on and that everything is neatly in its place. Why is it that we feel so uncomfortable about 'not knowing'. Why do we find silence and space so difficult. When we're together its common for people to keep talking at each other avoiding the possibility of deep connection and just skimming along the surface of reality in the world of thoughts, ideas and logic.

Open the window, abandon logic, try to stop making sense out of everything and just be with what is. Observe the ebb and flow of this cosmic dance. Stop finishing sentences and experiment with silence. Allow the word 'maybe' to be integrated into your mind on a deep level and try and avoid making definitive conclusions and judgments about the situations in life as they flash before your eyes. Instead of deciding that something is either good or bad, love or fear, light or shadow just try and be with what is. Be with what is without trying to translate it into any form or any thought.

Beyond our subjective realities and our self-created mind maps there is an objective universe that we all share. It is a place where we are all one, where we are all equal and a place we are all involved in. The only value we have in this place is our existence. We all exist equally and are all 'in the same boat'. There is no division, no borders, no me, no you... There is just 'Is-ness' – just now – just this.

'This' has no time, or place – or reason – it is without thought, without intention and without logic. It is here just because it is here. In this place there is no need for fear, everything is part of 'the way' and 'the way' is all there is.

Sharing, love and togetherness is the only thing that makes sense in this place of understanding as you are me and I am you. Finding this place can take time and its not always easy to sustain this perspective and perhaps it is not necessary all the time – its just nice when we are all united, in love and in peace. A good way to find this place is to play with perceptions, play with reality and see the changeable and transient nature of the mind, the emotions and the world of thoughts and ideas. Try and observe the fickle nature of that which changes and tune in to that which remains constant. This place in which we all dwell, this eternal 'now' – is what remains constant – free from ideas, thoughts, emotions and changes. It is all happening in the eternal now. We can experience emotions and thoughts as part of the now and that is fine, that is part of now – but being aware of how we are always in the same place, in the same time, in this eternal now can help us tune in to reality and find togetherness, love and union with the divine. Merging with this divine 'now' I feel is an act of 'Yoga' and it is one of the ways we can realize heaven.

'Hell' is the suffering caused by the disconnection and separation from 'now' – it is being lost in a place of isolation and delusion about the true nature of reality, seeing ourselves as separate entities responsible for our fate and all that happens to us. 'Heaven' is being aware of the way things really are and relaxing into pure presence. We are all in heaven, all of the time – heaven is our divine home and it is here and now. This world is a projection from the heavenly energy of consciousness and love and that power, that consciousness and love that this world is made of is 'all-powerful' it is the 'almighty', there is nothing greater.

Consider the intelligence behind snowflakes, butterflies, sunshine, rainbows, light and sound, colour and form. This intelligence effortlessly weaves its magic continuously in all of time and space. This is the intelligence that this world is made of and it is all-powerful. There is nothing to fear because the grip of power is complete and total, it is with pure consciousness and love energy. This whole universe is contained within that vibration. It is happening inside of this divine all-powerful light. In the same way that we dream at night and the dream happens inside our heads, this whole universe is happening inside the 'godhead'. When we have a bad dream we wake-up unharmed, complete and safe, resting in our bed safe and sound. This is the same for this universe, whatever can and will happen happens within the all-powerful expanse of consciousness and as a result no injury, harm loss or gain can happen. The power is constant.

I remember when I learned the law of thermodynamics in science at school which states that 'energy can never be created or destroyed, just transferred from one form to another' a light bulb switched on inside my head and I realised that there is no loss or gain. This universe is complete, so because of that there is just totality, oneness, perfection. Good and bad are just sides of the same coin, all judgments are just shadows that happen inside the totality of the one.

To some extent I feel I have touched this place of realizing the 'one consciousness' from which we all spring from. One of the strangest experiences I have ever had was when I was at a music festival. I was stood in the audience with my girlfriend and had been drinking a little bit and had smoked a joint. I was feeling the effects and suddenly felt an overwhelming need to lie down. I made my way to the side of the stage area and collapsed on the floor breathing heavily. I suddenly felt myself drifting in my awareness and drifting away from the festival and away from the being that I was. I melted and fell into an infinite ocean of bliss that was inside of me. I didn't leave my body, it wasn't like an outer-body experience but more a melting of my sense of self into a more expansive, infinite and blissful self. I felt a massive sense of peace, calm and contentment and remembered feeling that I couldn't believe how seriously I took the life that I was living as it was such a small part of the overall picture. I remember seeing a window of blue, almost like a TV screen showing the life that I had been living drifting away, getting smaller and smaller. I could still see all of the people and my girlfriend but it looked as though they were miles away on a small TV screen.

Surrounding the screen was white light in what felt like an expanse of infinite possibility. It seemed as though the life I had been living was more like a thought that had been explored by this infinite awareness, curious to explore the thought. It felt as though I was completely at peace, like desire and suffering had completely disappeared and there was absolutely no need for change of any kind, just complete and total contentment. But during all of this time I had been watching the small blue TV screen fading and getting smaller and noticed that in the window my girlfriend was getting hysterical and looked distressed. I remember feeling that I could not leave her to deal with my body and that I must force my way back into being. At the time it seemed like the hardest thing in the world to do, to bring myself back into being. If you imagine being in a large room filled with objects and possibilities and that in this large room you notice a crumb on the table at the far end of the room, that was what the blue window looked like to me. It felt as though the only way I could bring myself back into my body was to focus all of my attention on this crumb and see nothing more, so that I could fit back into my 'Stuart' shaped hole in the fabric of eternity. I pushed and focused and centered my awareness solely on the small blue window until I was gripped by it, and had re-aligned with it. I came back into my body and felt very cold; I had to beat my legs to get them to work and the first thing I said to my girlfriend was 'I know why people are in comas, because they view this life as though it is a dream and they no longer have control over it', I think this was a realization of how life really is a dream and when people get into a coma state they have just slipped into the 'dreaming' state which is the real origin of this life. It was a very strange experience and I think it was more than just the effects of the joint as I have smoked lots of times in my life and the experience I had was far more than anything I had experienced before when smoking. My girlfriend said at one point my lips went blue and she really thought I had 'gone', it certainly seemed that way to me.

This experience to me points to the idea that we all stem from one universal mind that it is nothing but pure consciousness and that if attention is given to a thought by the universal mind than that thought can be explored and so form is born from the universal mind as a mechanism of god-like imagination power that playfully aides the exploration of a thought within the expanse of infinite consciousness. It seemed to me that the only way I could 'be' was to fix my attention on 'the story of Stuart' so that the story may continue to unfold.

In conclusion, my experience of reality has been fluid, not

fixed. There is a shared 'true' reality which has the power to unite us all if we surrender to it and melt into the dance, and there is also a personal, changeable and fickle reality which we create and maintain. Perceptions and experiences are things which can evolve and change based on our awareness. There is much more to this world then we know or could ever know in words and ideas. The world is what it is, it is its own answer and also it is the question. It is the beginning and the end. If the universe was a sentence of words then that sentence would be the meaning of life. 'Cogito ergo sum' – I think, therefore I am.

HIPPIE LIFESTYLE

Any fully fledged hippie will probably at some point decide that the oppressive capitalist game that society plays, filled with rules and restrictions is not really for them and as such will seek to find 'another way'. Either that or they might charge at society head-on and seek to create change from the inside, which can be a very noble approach. Either way, hippies are generally pretty alternative creatures who drift on the outskirts of mainstream society in search of something more sacred, natural and uplifting. As a fully-fledged hippie myself I can suggest a few things that might appeal to any up-and-coming hippies as ways of existing in the world and getting-by whilst still managing to follow the heartfelt vibe of 'the hippie'.

One of the most difficult things for most aspiring hippies is the money problem, paying bills, buying food etc. It might be common for the hippie to try and allow themselves to have as much free time as possible so that they might pursue heart-felt dreams that often don't pay so well such as music, art, charity, and most other nice things – seems strange doesn't it that we often reward the most immoral jobs with the highest pay – as though we are actually making a deal with the devil or something... So, hippies might opt for low-pay, part time work or try and get by on whatever they can get. This can be possible, and I have known LOTS of people who manage this way – Busking can be a great way to earn extra money if your hard-up and can perform something in the streets, you could play guitar, sing, juggle, dance, read poetry or do some groovy psychedelic performance art in the streets. Iv known people who can earn around £60-100 per night busking. I once lived off the proceeds I made from busking. I used to dress up in a purple suit and a top hat with bright yellow sunglasses and go door-to-door charging £1 per song. It was a truly magical experience, I met some lovely people, sang to quite a few lonely house-bound people, and generally brightened up a lot of peoples days and earned on average £10 per hour. You may need to get a peddlers license in the UK if you decide to go door-to-door, you can get them from the council for about £12 per year.

Another way to try and solve the money problem so that you can spend your days daydreaming and exploring consciousness is to focus your efforts on generating 'passive-income;. This is the type of income which just arrives to you without you having to do anything. There is usually an initial investment of time and energy and then you can just reap the rewards, pay your bills and float on the winds of the cosmic rainbow. The internet has given us a vast array of ways to earn passive income, such as blogging, uploading videos, self-publishing your book or music, adsense, selling your skills via video tutorials, selling digital products such as video and mp3 files etc etc... I personally do a combination of these things to help bring in some magic beans so that I can just flip-flop down the stairway of life like a purple slinky spring. Famous people who might have made it in the music world often just live off royalties... that's why they can often be complete space cadets and still manage to pay their bills throughout their lives, just one hit song could set you up for life.

Another idea for ways of getting by is to become a live-in volunteer at a community – or join the Wwoof scheme – and work in exchange for food and board. I did this for four years, it was great, I met a lot of people and didn't have to think about bills or money for the whole time which was incredibly liberating. There are lots of places all around the world who accept volunteers. Some of the more interesting places can be retreat centers, there you will often encounter many a like mind and find fellow hippies to hang out with.

You could also try living without money at all – and maybe doing a combination of squatting, living in a tree-house or a cave (I know someone who lived in the beach caves in Ibiza) and 'Freeganism' which is what you call the practice of eating waste food from large supermarkets who often throw out all of their unwanted but perfectly edible food with expired sell by dates. There are a number of communities filled with people who live without money and just get by on the grace of god. Two places that I can think of are 'Tipi Valley' in Wales in the UK – and 'Beneficio' in Granada in Spain. These are large plots of land where people live in yurts, tipi's, tents, roundhouses and treehouses. Iv been to Tipi Valley and stayed for about a week, it seemed pretty nice. I stayed in the 'Big Lodge' which is a giant tipi that they have for visitors to stay in free of charge. It is only semi-communal as everyone kind of just does their own thing but at least everyone is more or less on the same page in that they all want to live close to the earth and in a kinda tribe. Living in the woods in a tent isn't really for me though, iv lived in a caravan once that's about as close as iv got to that and on the whole I prefer living in buildings that are water-proof with running water and drainage.

You could try and become a monk and devote your life to meditation and spiritual practice and maybe live in a monastery. Most of the monks I have met in my life are quite hippie-ish... they are often quite chilled out, loving and laid back self-aware types – although when I went to India I went and stayed for a while at a large Tibetan settlement full of monks and I was surprised to see them riding around on Harley Davidsons, covered in tattoos and drinking cans of coca cola. They also seemed quite un-friendly – but I guess they were in exile so perhaps that was why, anyway, I learnt you cant judge a book by its cover.

Maybe you could form a music band, pour your love in to it and make it big so that you dont have to be a slave to the system anymore and with all of your wealth you could set up a big hippie commune. If you cant make it famous you could try and round up as many hippies as you can to create a commune, pool all of your resources and wealth so that your shared power helps to make life easier for all. Its surprising how easy life can get when you live in a collective and everyone shares the work-load. From my experience communal living vastly enhances ones quality of life and I would recommend it to anyone. I feel that we are naturally tribal creatures who need to live in packs and I feel that the communal approach, living symbiotically, is completely in tune with natures way.

Perhaps you could just decide that the world is your home and go traveling with a tent or staying on people's sofas. You could hitch hike and meet lots of people and see where the wind takes you. You could devote your time to nurturing the earth, planting trees, loving people and getting involved in random acts of kindness and compassion.

Another option would be to buy an old bus, paint it bright colours and turn it in to a hippie fun bus and go on a magical mystery tour. This is something iv wanted to do for years but as of yet haven't managed to do. A great way to do it would be to form a band and try and go on a musical tour at the same time, playing gigs at various places on your travels whilst taking camping detours out into the woods and excursions to various towns and cities meeting people and exploring life.

Failing all of that you could just try and start a hippie

revolution so that the whole world tuns on to the power of love and then we can all live in harmony, as one, forevermore. One day I feel that flower power will blossom and bloom into a magical mandala of loveliness and we will all see that with the power of our hearts we can share heaven and peace.

COSMIC CONSCIOUSNESS

Hippies are known to have an interest in mind expansion and generally be quite spiritual. They like to see beyond borders and walls, look around corners and try and discover the unknown. Seeking enlightenment is a common goal of the hippie. Enlightenment is generally pretty hard to define or understand but as far as I am aware it is the deep acceptance of that which has always been and always will be and an awareness of the 'true self'. Meditation is often thought to be one of the key processes to encourage this state of enlightenment and it is practiced by many monks and pilgrims all around the world.

Tuning in to 'now' is a great way to understand life. Some people think that the activation of the third eye is an important part in expanding consciousness and becoming more enlightened. The third eye in the brain is the Pineal gland, a cone shaped gland located in the middle of the brain just above the pituitary gland. It contains a pigment similar to that found in the eyes and is said to control the action of light upon our body. Personally I remember when I became aware of my third eye. It was after spending 10 days with Don Conreaux on the Gongmaster training course, playing gongs, practicing sacred ceremonies and raising our vibrational energies. After the 10 days I began to feel a pulsing on my forehead just between my eyes. I felt 'grounded' and 'present' and calm. My personality seemed to change. It was quite a strange experience. I still can feel the pulsing to this day and often I meditate upon it – it feels to me like a small window of opportunity for my awareness to link with a consciousness that transcends my body. The pulsing is like a data link – or radio receiver transmitting and receiving this gentle wave-like pulse. I don't really know what it is for but I know that I like it and it seems to give me a sense of calm.

Getting to grips with some of our most popular esoteric/new age philosophies is useful for the modern day hippie and it will help you to link with your tribe. Learning about aura's, chakaras and astral bodies is a good place to start – so here is a quick rough guide to hippie new age philosophy.

Our body is thought to have 7 main chakras - The seven chakras are the centers in which cosmic energy flows through and they are the 7 colours of the rainbow. Blocked energy in our seven chakras is thought to cause illness, whereas activation of the chakra is linked to health and vitality.

1. Root Chakra – Colour RED - Located in base of spine - Survival issues such as financial independence, money and food.

2. Sacral Chakra – Colour ORANGE - Located lower back/lower abdomen - Sense of abundance, well-being, pleasure and sexuality.

3. Solar Plexus Chakra – Colour YELLOW - Located in stomach area – feelings of self-worth, self-confidence and self-esteem.

4. Heart Chakra – Colour GREEN - Our ability to love, feel joy and inner peace.

5. Throat Chakra – Colour BLUE - Our ability to communicate, site for expression of feelings and the truth.

6. Third Eye Chakra – Colour PURPLE - Located on the Forehead between the eyes, Intuition, imagination, wisdom

7. Crown Chakra – Colour WHITE - Located at The very top of the head. The highest chakra, our connection to spirituality and pure bliss.

The body is also thought to have many layers - The physical body and The astral body. The astral body is an aura of swirling changing colours. It is an electromagnetic energy field which surrounds the body and which is often thought to have a colour depending on how you are feeling and what vibrations you are sending out and receiving. It is linked with out-of-body experiences and astral projection. Astral projection is a willful out-of-body experience that projects ones soul or consciousness throughout the universe. You can observe the aura using an electromagnetic field monitor and can actually see what colour your aura is. You can also use a machine to show you the health and status of all of your chakras. I had mine monitored once, apparently most of mine were quite small at the time, apart from my third eye, which was unusually large, I think it was around the time I went on that gong course, so it seemed to make sense.

Sacred Geometry is another interesting area of life to

consider. It is well documented and understood that there is some kind of 'Divine Order' within the universe and apparently all objects throughout the universe are bound by a mathematical perfection. Its as though the universe is like a magic mandala that is perfectly unfolding. Just look at a snowflake and consider the magic and intelligence which caused such a thing to exist.

I believe a mandala can say so much. These magic shapes are like the primal language of the universe itself. Dr Emoto's discoveries about the way thoughts, intentions and vibrations effect the shape and formation of water crystals show to me that the language of mandala's is the language of this universe. Our vibrations are translated by this universe in to shapes, mandala's and patterns. Another trippy thought is – 'are the patterns we see happening inside or outside of ourselves?' - because we can only ever experience that which has first been passed through our senses – we can only in essence ever experience ourselves and whatever reflections of reality we create inside of ourselves. The instrument we use to translate, perceive and experience this world is our body, brains and mind. So anything we experience is a reflection of that. These patterns that we see, may not be the full picture, they might just represent what we are capable of seeing and understanding.... who knows?

All of this stuff is in some way important and from personal experience the status of your energy centers can have a profound effect on your experience of reality – but personally I feel that this information is only a signpost towards the 'holy grail' – it is just part of the changeable world of things that come and go – whereas the holy grail is the place where everything stays the same, where we are all one and where there is only love, peace, silence, emptiness and completeness. Satcitananda .

सच्चिदानन्द

ॐ भूर्भुवः स्वः
तत्सवितुर्वरेण्यं
भर्गो देवस्य धीमहि
धियो योनःप्रचोदयात्

MEDITATION

ॐ ॐ

Meditation is a fundamental part of learning to harmonize with the self, and the universe. I believe that meditation is a natural process and many people go into various states of meditation naturally, throughout the day. I do however believe that it is important to go through a formal process of sitting down to meditate regularly to build up the strength of ones relationship with the art of meditating and beginning to assimilate the teachings of meditation in to your daily life. I believe that ultimately life itself is one long and profound meditation that is being expressed through the consciousness of the universe and that each person is a mediation.

So, where to begin with meditation? Well, its great to start by making a regular time to sit down in peace and quiet for about 30 mins in a group or on your own. Sit comfortably, close your eyes and just 'be'. Pay attention to all of the processes and dynamics that are occurring within your consciousness and within your living experience. Pay attention to your breathing, the buzz and energy of being alive, your body heat, your ever changing tapestry of thoughts, your heart beat, the wind on your face, the hum in your ears. Pay attention to all of the memories that flash through your mind, to the desires and urges, the pain and the joy. The art of meditation is largely based around your ability to tune in to the constant consciousness that underpins all changeable phenomena, put simply to become aware of your awareness and just simply 'be'. To find a deep acceptance in all of the changing states that occur in your experience and find that which remains constant.

Meditation has completely changed my perspective on life and also my experience. I believe that really getting to grips with meditation and what it is trying to teach will help you to unlock your power, your true potential and in some ways your magic. Understanding the dynamics of life and this universe is so much more important then virtually everything else. Society, being rich, being famous, being attractive, having possessions, being 'somebody', being 'intelligent', filling your mind with facts and information or having big muscles is all ultimately unimportant and to chase any of these is just a distraction from the main issue that life presents. The deep questions that we all have about life act as our signposts to intuitively follow so that we can find our way home, reach 'Nirvana' and find heaven here on Earth. The key to all of our joy, peace, love and energetic harmony can be found through meditation. No 'thing' in the world could ever offer a permanent solution to peace and love because all material phenomena, everything in this material world is subject to change, to cycles of birth and death. To try and rely on anything in the world as a solution to happiness is inevitably setting yourself up for pain as all things will pass and that thing that your using as your solution will one day pass, including all the people you love and everything that you hold on to for sanctuary and a sense of self and identity. There is one thing however, which doesn't pass, and which doesn't change, and that something is what meditation is trying to show you. That something is essentially what you are, it is the something that you have been all along, that something which is beyond time, space, form and change. It also transcends all birth and death and remains constant. If you place your mind in this place, your true home, you will find lasting peace and all of the changes that take place around you will begin to loose their power as you find your never ending inner peace. You will begin to see that all things change, all things pass, and that 'you' essentially stay the same through all the changes. You will in essence 'wake up' from the dream of 'self'. Meditation is a big deal, and can lead you to true liberation.

So what are these lessons that we are trying to learn in life? Well, I have noticed that all so called lessons that we are learning all point to the art of 'letting go' of 'chilling out' about things. What does that really mean? Well, letting go means to let go of our attachments and fall backwards into the ocean of infinite peace that resides in our hearts. Learning to accept is a form of letting go, chilling out and so on. Its all pointing to one thing, to just be what you are, be free from notions of self, of identity and filled with attachments. Its actually the easiest thing you can do in life, to simply let go, but because it is so easy it is hard. Hard to believe that we don't need to fix everything and do everything ourselves, that the world wont turn unless we make it, that we are not the center of the universe and our legacy is all-important. This thing we call our 'Ego' causes us a lot of suffering because it is subject to constant rejection and is never given the credit that it feels it deserves as it is never ending. The Ego's ultimate goal is world domination, to become godlike – and maybe even become the one ruler of the universe. It gives us a sense of self-importance and on the flip-side, pain and anguish because it is not getting what it wants. This is all ok, and doesn't matter – its just part of the human experience and in the end becomes quite humorous.

As I was growing up I began to realise all of the things that I don't do in this world, rather then think about the things that I do. There is so very much that I don't do, and that I can just experience and observe. The clouds in the sky drift by without my input, the birds sing, the grass grows, people are born and die, the cells in my hand grow and repair, the sun burns, the planets turn, the water flows, insects make their little nests, my heart beats, people fall in love, have dreams and form friendships, all this happens outside of my will, and without me having to do anything. The world doesn't really need me to function, it can do that without my help. This notion can feel a bit deflating, like, 'oh, all this time I thought I was doing it all, I thought that the world couldn't exist without me' – but then, it is also so very liberating. You can just sit back, almost on your metaphorical sun-lounger and just chill out and feel the warmth of the rays of life shine upon your consciousness like sunlight. Just allow life to help you grow like a flower grows in the sunshine. We really can 'let go' and relax, and just let life do its thing.

Meditation is all about this kind of thing. Learning to accept on a deep non-intellectual way, that the way things are, is the way things are. That there is no alternative, and that it is all deeply intelligent and functional and that we can 'trust'. Acceptance and letting go doesn't mean apathy either, we don't just become like despondent zombies allowing the world to do whatever it likes to us without responding. Deep acceptance includes accepting that sometimes you don't agree, that sometimes you might feel anger, that sometimes you feel pain and suffering. One of the first Buddhist precepts is to accept that there is suffering, I believe that this notion is very profound. Yes, there is suffering, that is the way it is. So why freak out about anything? 'it is the way it is' ..... 'thy will be done on Earth as it is in heaven' - Heaven is in the heart, and it shines its light into this world - so what is in heaven will be done here on earth. Heaven is what you are.

So anyway, a good place to start with meditation is to sit every day, for about 30 mins, even 10 mins if you find that 30 is too many. And just pay attention to everything, watching things arise and pass, arise and pass, be born and die. Thoughts are born, then they die. The song of a bird is born, then when it stops, it is dead. This is life.

Then try just tuning in to your breath, just breathe. Feel your breath, feel it deeply, the rising and the falling of the belly. Y'know a good tip, you can trick your body into feeling relaxed by just breathing properly, breathe consciously with your belly, this activates certain neuronal pathways in your spine which tell your brain that you are relaxed, releasing endorphin's and making you feel nice. Just breathe, when your in situations in life just continue to observe, allow, accept and breathe. Eventually the way of meditation will be integrated into your daily life and you will practice the same dynamics in waking life.

Another really useful and good thing to meditate on is the zen koan 'Who Am I' – simply ask yourself this question in your mind, over and over again. Mediate on this question, not trying to seek a defined answer but just being open, keep on asking 'who am I'. I found that in stressful situations in life asking myself 'who am I' and becoming aware of my breathe helped me to relax.

It is also good to relax in to your authentic self, into your freedom. You don't have to make sense, to do what everyone else is doing, you don't have to speak if you don't feel like it, or respond appropriately. If someone tells you 'my uncle has just died' you don't have to be sad if you don't feel sad. We spend so much time faking it, doing what we 'should' be doing and being polite that we forget who we really are and get lost in a fuzz of stressful social interactions. Its good to find your freedom, to relax in to 'being' – if you can genuinely relax and feel free, you will help others to see that they are also allowed to be themselves and operate freely. The grip of logic over our interactions can be crippling, we are all trying to make sense all the time. Look at the universe, it flows, it is colorful, nature is illogical and flowing – not so many rigid lines and order. Learn your timeless, free, illogical self and shine like the sun. relaxing in to our authentic self can also help us with our meditation. But beware not to become obsessed with our own journey either at the expense of all others. Yeah, its complicated, but also, extremely simple.

"You should sit in meditation for at least 20 mins every day, unless you are too busy, then you should sit for at least an hour" - Old Zen saying...

YOGA

What is Yoga? and how does the practice of Yoga aim to improve our experience of life and our interaction and relationship with the physical world around us?......

Often in life it is common for people to look outside of themselves for fulfillment and satisfaction. We are living in a society that encourages us generally to believe that outer attainments can provide us with what we want and satisfy our souls. Yet time and time again our experiences often lead us to feel that nothing external can completely satisfy the deep yearning within for "something more." Most of our actions seem to be guided by a striving for that which is just beyond our reach, over the hill and far away. Most people are seemingly caught up in a perpetual cycle of 'doing' rather than 'being' and are often concerned with performing actions rather than being anchored in awareness. For a lot of people contentment and complete calmness is difficult to imagine. Yet calmness and peace allows us to engage fully with life and experience a state of bliss and contentment which is difficult to achieve when striving for it.... Letting go is actually easier then performing actions yet it seems most people believe that one must strive towards a feeling of contentment and peace rather then just let go and sink into the peace and contentment that is already present within ourselves i.e. 'there is no mountain to climb, you are already sat on the top'

Yoga is an ancient spiritual science which offers a direct means of stilling the natural turbulence of thoughts and restlessness of the mind and body that prevents us from knowing and fully experiencing what we really are.

Ordinarily our perceptions and awareness is focused on outward things in the world around us and our experience of the world is dominated by the signals we receive from the limited channels of our five senses. Most of our thought processes and our logic and reasoning often relies upon the partial and often incomplete data supplied by the physical senses, So, one of the tasks of yoga is to try and go beyond the senses and go deeper, into a state that is steady, that does not change and is beyond a need for reason, logic, interpretation and understanding, into a place that just 'is' so that then we may know the self and begin to answer or at least feel understanding for the big questions in life such as – Who am I? and Why am I here?

The word Yoga means "union": referring to the union of the individual consciousness with the Universal Consciousness. Yoga is a method used to try and create a state of 'union' - a state of oneness with the senses, the self, the world and all worlds, both inner and outer. It is a practice that can calm the mind and allow a person to step beyond desire and beyond needs. It is a process that helps to purify our energies and harmonise us with nature and the universe and allow us to see, feel and experience the wonder and sacred truth that is life itself. Yoga can tune us in to a deep and sacred natural intelligence that is present in all.

The traditional materialistic idea of life has generally vanished with the discovery that matter and energy are essentially one: every part of this wondrous universe can be observed on a sub-atomic level as a sacred geometrical pattern or form of energy, which interacts and interconnects us with other forms resulting in one great sea of energy and consciousness separated only through our own individual sense perceptions.

It is common for people to think that Yoga is purely a physical exercises but the postures or 'Asanas' are actually only the most superficial aspect to this profound science of the human mind and soul.

There are various pathways one can become involved with when practicing Yoga, and often people blend many of them together to practice in their daily lives.

Hatha Yoga – a system of physical postures designed to purify the body and allow for greater bodily awareness creating optimum conditions for meditation.

Karma Yoga – selfless service to others as part of one's larger universal Self, letting go of any attachment to the results; and becoming aware that the performance of all actions can be attributed to the universal consciousness of the infinite universe often referred to as God..

Mantra Yoga – A process of centering and focusing the

attention by repeating 'japa' or mantras i.e. a series of word sounds and phrases spoken or sang repetitively.

Bhakti Yoga – all-surrendering devotion and selfless service through which one attempts to see and love the divinity in every creature and in everything.

Jnana (Gyana) Yoga – the path of wisdom, which emphasizes the importance of selective intelligence and reason to achieve spiritual liberation and understanding of the true higher self.

Raja Yoga – Used by the Indian sage Patanjali, it is a form of yoga which attempts to combine the essence of all the other paths.

May your path towards liberation and truth be strong, blessed and filled with compassion, love and divinity. May the long time sunshine shine upon you.

Love, love, love.

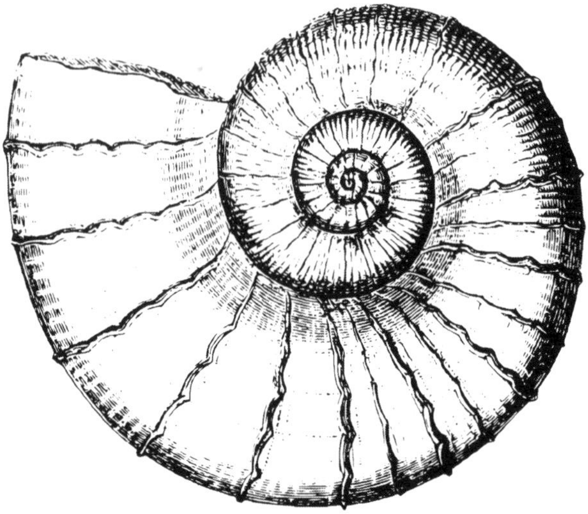

PSYCHEDELIC SPACEMAN

In my own life I have had many experiences over the years with various forms of mind alterations and expansions. I Think it is only natural to explore reality and to have a great sense of wonder about the mind and what it is capable of and also feel a great yearning to begin to find answers and understanding for some of the bigger questions in life such as 'why am I here' 'is there a god' and 'is life just a dream'. I think part of this quest for truth often leads us to experiment with certain mind altering drugs in the hope that it might reveal some answers or maybe connect us deeper with 'god' or 'nature' or 'the universe'.

During the psychedelic 60's there was a huge interest in mind expanding substances and they flooded our streets and our popular culture. Our music was heavily influenced by the use of drugs and so was our taste in clothes. The Doors, Jimi Hendrix, The Beatles and many more were all users of various psychedelic substances such as L.S.D, Pot, Psilocybin, Mescaline and more. Some people in the 60's and 70's believed that L.S.D was a direct and quick route to finding enlightenment and just one acid trip could reveal to the user the most profound secrets behind this universe and consciousness. There were many people during the 60's and 70's who treated the consumption of L.S.D as sacred and indeed spent their time promoting and encouraging people to do it in order to discover enlightenment in the hope of creating a more harmonious and enlightened world. Ken Kesey and the Merry Pranksters were one such group of individuals. They lived communally at Kesey's place's in California and Oregon, and are remembered for a lengthy road trip they took in the summer of 64' traveling across the USA in a bright and colourful psychedelic painted school bus called 'Furthur or Further', organizing parties and encouraging people to take the 'Acid Test'. Timothy Leary was another major proponent of L.S.D, an American psychologist and writer who was one of the first scientists to conduct experiments backed by Harvard University with L.S.D and Psilocybin and is known for advocating the exploration of the therapeutic potential of psychedelic drugs. He later abandoned the restrictive idea's of society and the university, went to live in a large hippie commune, created a kind of cult and was the first to coin the phrase 'Turn on, Tune in and Drop out'. There were many more major players in the psychedelic movement including one of Timothy Leary's assistants Richard Alpert – who in the 60's took some acid and decided to drop out of society, quit his career, change his name to 'Ram Dass' and move to India to worship a spiritual teacher named Maharishi Mahesh Yogi. He later became a well known speaker and writer, a book entitled 'Be Here Now' being one of his principle works, its a good book, very hippiefied, i'd recommend it.

Aldous Huxley is another big name in the world of mind alteration - 'The Doors of Perception' is a book, by Aldous Huxley which details his experiences when taking mescaline (obtained from the Pyote cactus). Its a fascinating book which describes in detail how heightened his perceptions became and how time seemed to dissolve in to infinity. 'The Doors' the music band, named themselves after his book. Someone who is close to me once told me a story about how they ingested some mescaline and spent the entire day watching a silver-birch tree rattle its leaves in the wind and he said that he felt as though the tree was talking to him and when in this state of awareness he felt as though he could understand what the tree was saying.

I love how sometimes altered states can put us in touch with nature and break us free from the logical order of the societal flow. Iv never had Mescaline myself, or L.S.D but iv always had a certain romanticism about it and feel a calling from within to expand my consciousness and reach a greater understanding of the universe, so I can sympathize with anyone who tries this particular route to expand their mind.

Using psychedelic substances has been a long-standing traditional thing for some peoples and some cultures. Shamanism is one such tradition where the use of psychedelics a.k.a 'Plant Medicines' is commonplace and many rituals and ceremonies use the plant medicines to aide a healing process deep within human consciousness. Ayahuasca is one such plant that has rapidly become a trend among a new generation of 'seekers' from the west who are looking to find enlightenment and healing. It has been used as a healing medicine by shamans in forest tribes for generations. Ayahuasca is believed to open up a portal to the spirit world and can project your consciousness into a different realm of reality. Traditionally an Ayahuasca healing ceremony involves ingesting the substance in the form of a brew and then the shaman leading the ceremony will sing sacred songs to you and guide you through the landscape of the spirit world so that you may discover the deep dynamics of your mind, subconscious and the world of spirit and resolve any issues on this level so that you can be healed and enlightened. Ayahuasca is likely to make you vomit and have diarrhea and people believe that this purging also helps to cleanse the body and remove unwanted energies and toxins. Iv heard that the experience of taking Ayahuasca is both deeply pleasant and unpleasant and quite full-on, iv never actually tried it, but i'm open minded and maybe some day if I find myself somewhere deep in the Amazon jungle with a trippy tribe of magic shaman people I might give it a try. I believe that using psychedelic plants as a form of medicine is probably the best way of relating to the use of psychedelics. I believe that maybe by having this intimate relationship with plants, nature and our consciousness we can learn more about ourselves and the world we live in and perhaps 'tune in' more to the subtle flow of peaceful cosmic vibrations.

When I was growing up during my teenage years 'pot' was

often on the menu. Being stoned was the thing to do when I was a teenager and all of my friends were doing it. I probably spent the majority of my evenings being stoned for years when I was growing up. So, did I learn anything from this strange plant? Well, I think one thing that 'weed' can teach you is how suggestible and powerful thoughts and mind states can be on your perception and experience of reality. If I had negative thoughts when I was stoned it could lead to a complete collapse of the self and a retreat in to some kind of cave within my consciousness. Negative thoughts and suggestions could cause great anxiety and fear and be very disabling – causing what is known as a 'Whitey'. This happened to me quite a bit when I was young. But conversely, when I was exposed to positive thoughts and suggestions it would elevate me to great joyous heights and I would be laughing endlessly and feeling bliss-ed out. Pot can also enhance ones awareness of the solar plexus and make you aware of this energy center and how to control your sense of peace by letting go. I think pot can also help your mind to embrace the illogical and disregard the importance of logic and order that is often taught to us in schools and by our society and governments (N.B. Did you know that the word government actually means 'mind control' in Latin? 'ment = mind' in Latin). I think pot can encourage a more laid back and humorous approach to life. I'm not saying that this kind of approach can only be learned through smoking pot, but it is something that maybe I learned.

Other drugs that were floating around when I was younger included the synthetic drugs cocaine, ecstasy & speed - my experience of these drugs is fairly limited but I was never really a fan of the 'unnatural' drugs. The high seemed a bit too unnatural and unhealthy. Some of the heightened feelings of 'love' from ecstasy were quite interesting though, as I once remember being in a large city rave full of gangster types but because everyone was high, everyone was lovely and hugging each other. I hugged a huge gangster man who offered to give me his huge gold chain and told me how we're all connected and we're all one. Kinda nice, but there's something 'unreal' about these synthetic highs and I didn't really learn anything per say.

A very strange drug experience I had involved the use of the shamanistic herb 'Salvia Divinorum' which at the time was legal and could be bought online. It was one of the strongest most potent hallucinogenic drugs I have ever experienced. I smoked some of this stuff and it completely turned my world upside down and inside out – I was in my living room at the time but on the trip I thought that I was sat backstage with a group of people waiting to get up and perform some music. I was also looking at my carpet which looked like a beach and I could see the sea lapping up on the shore from a kind of birds-eye view. I then fell backwards and started eating a strawberry sky whilst a bunch of playing cards, kings and queens, started dancing around me. It was intense, and strange. The main high lasts about 15 mins but the after effects can last for a few days. The following day was pretty awful, I felt like I was out of my body and it took me all day to opon a tin of tomatoes with a can opener, I had to keep on going back to bed and having breaks. How I can describe it is that if life is you pulling yourself along by holding on to a rope, it felt as though I had lost my grip on this rope and could no longer function. Luckily the effect wore off after a day. My close friend also had the same effect and apparently spent the day as a passenger in a car on a long journey trying to eat the road as it was moving towards him. The only thing that I may have learned from this drug was that maybe I caught a glimpse of some kind of strange alternate reality as this message was the same for all the people I was with. It felt as though life was a stage, and everything that happens is scripted, known, pre-planned and that we are all characters just acting out our part. It also felt as though there was an audience watching me. My audience was applauding and laughing luckily. Perhaps this audience is my psyche, my subconscious....who knows....

During my fourth year in the hippie commune when things

were staring to kind of fall apart, everything got quite difficult to deal with. We happened to live in the countryside surrounded by fields and during September-October time the fields were full of magic mushrooms. Well, as a kind of instinct to self medicate I had a number of low doses on quite a number of occasions. From my experience I have always found magic mushrooms pretty easy to handle and very positive. They helped me to remember the deep ocean of peace that swirls around in my solar plexus, helped me to not take everything so seriously and to see the funny side of things and also they seemed to make me extra aware of magnetic fields around my body and my spine. The doses I was taking (between 10 and 30 mushrooms) seemed to be medicinal to me and from what I can gather scientists are starting to see that in low doses mushrooms are good for your nervous system and can help to combat depression and stimulate the growth of new neurons and new neuronal pathways. Overall and so far they have been a very positive experience for me. They do seem like they could potentially be very strong if taken in large quantities but this is something iv never done.

One thing I remember about mushrooms is that they can help to show you how to think in ways that you don't normally think in. I remember I was once lay in the bath on mushrooms and it felt as though I was in the ocean under a tropical sea, it was bliss, I closed my eyes, dunked my head under water and started to think in 4D. I was thinking in shapes, not in words. I was thinking of the shape of a starfish – but in a very vivid and strange way that's hard to describe. On the whole I have a kind of friendly attitude towards mushrooms, I think when treated responsibly, they can perhaps be good for you.

My overall feeling on drugs is that they are only signposts towards the ultimate truths. Chasing any kind of experience will only give you temporary satisfaction and will not give you a long-lasting sense of 'knowledge'. It is quite common for people to seek answers through experiences but my recommendation would be to seek that which does not change, which cannot come and go, that which you already own. To know this will bring you a deep sense of understanding and lasting peace.

There are many other ways to expand ones consciousness and open our minds to divine cosmic energies and tune ourselves into and become able to speak the language of the universe. Through meditation, yoga, moral integrity, clean living, love, kindness and open-warmheartedness we can alter our consciousness and start to experience this world in many different ways. I have had first hand experience of just how trippy the world can become even when one is sober.

First I would suggest listening to your heart and trying to find honesty, humility and with an open heart try to understand what it is you really want. The answer to what you want will probably be 'peace and love' – so, how do you go about finding this. Cultivate a strong, rooted and committed spiritual outlook and use your heart as a compass to navigate your way down the path of soul realization. Try and consider the idea that life is sacred, it has a purpose (in a sense) which is divine, holy and intelligent. This life and this earth is a sacred temple for the soul, it is the most sacred tool that we know of for the soul to find its way towards actualization. Try to become aware of the life force and the pulsing rhythms and cycles of this sacred holy mandala that is our universe. Sense consciousness, in yourself, in the air, in the trees, in the rocks, in the silence. Sense that presence in both things and non-things. When your spiritual practice is real, rooted, honest and committed perhaps you could start to create rituals and get involved in practices that enhance your sacred sense.

Building a little shine in your room, or indeed a whole temple if you can, is a great way to keep focus and to keep you reminded of your commitment to mind and soul expansion, and your calling for cosmic consciousness. A temple or a shine is a little bit like a portal or a space-ship for our consciousness to use so that it may connect and travel into the timeless swirling unknown. We can use rituals, spirituality and objects to help strengthen our understanding of that which transcends our logical day-to-day experience. Through my own practices I have reached very strange levels and states of being – I have sensed the presence of powerful divine energies and felt a soul-level communication with the spirit-world. I have used my soul energy to speak directly to another persons soul and have experienced a disintegration in the fabric of time. Iv seen that reality is not as linear and logical as we often believe and that time is not so rigid. The appearance of things is largely held in place by our minds and our beliefs. If you have seen the film 'The Never Ending Story' well, from my own experience, reality is a bit like it is in this film. We are living in 'Fantasia' – a world that can only exist through the power of our own beliefs. Through our collective consciousness we keep alive this dream and we co-create how it feels and looks. In schools we are taught what 'things' are, how they look and sound and we are taught to logically define our world in such a way, This is a kind of mind programming where we are passing on a model for reality so that our children can then use this model to translate the energies of the universe into that version of reality. Well, it is much more fluid, you can change the way you see the world, and it will literally change before your eyes 'beauty is in the eye of the beholder'.

There is that physics experiment where they discovered that an object only exists when it is being observed, and when it is not being observed the energy that made that object instead of being defined, becomes everywhere in the universe, it becomes dispersed energy, not defined energy. So, we have scientific proof that our mind and our interactions with the energy of the universe cause it to be defined and solid, as we see it, but when we look away, that energy is free and undefined. If we change our definitions we change what we see. What im trying to say is, reaching altered states and contacting divine energies is entirely possible with the power of your own mind. Flow like the water and be at one with the ocean.

BEING VEGETARIAN/VEGAN

One of the first things that arose for me when I had this deep desire for peace was that I wanted to stop eating meat. It was quite a powerful and memorable experience that has stuck with me – I was about 15 and was living at home with my family who all ate meat and thought nothing of it. One day I was in the kitchen and I was making my own dinner – and I was preparing a chicken leg and was trying to tear the meat off the bone to be added to something I was making. I was looking at the chicken leg and my hands and all of a sudden became more and more aware of what I was doing – I could see tendons, I could see skin and bone and could hear the fleshy squelching sounds and see the gristle of fat – it looked horrific and my heart started to race and was pounding very strongly, I started sweating and had to sit outside. I realised the reality of what I was doing in that moment. It was like a scene from a horror movie – I was literally ripping apart a leg with my hands like a monster, In that moment I stopped eating meat and I believe it was one of the first steps in my spiritual awakening.

Not eating meat has evolved for me more and more over the years and now I am so glad that the magnetism of my heart lead me to make that choice. I am now a vegan and I now know more about the horror and abuse that animals face all around the world and am so glad that I am doing my best to avoid contributing to the suffering of these poor creatures. I feel that I am living more respectfully towards the earth, towards life and my relationship with the great spirit is improved because I am respecting her.

Being vegetarian and vegan I believe is a spiritual practice that helps you connect more deeply with nature and the earth. It helps you to feel at peace with animals and I feel that animals generally trust me more and respect me more because I respect them. I have never been stung by a bee, and I personally attribute this to my peaceful relationship with nature and animals (im not saying its a sign that your a good or bad person if you have been stung, its just a personal thought I have about myself).

I believe that to be a peaceful person in this world one must seek to minimise any suffering that they cause to other people and other beings of earth and avoid being violent. The meat industry is laden with deep deep suffering and violence and I believe that if you take part in this cycle of suffering you will attract bad karma into your own life. I also feel that if people ingest pain and suffering they will inevitably feel that pain in their own bodies. I can tell if someone is a vegetarian or vegan just from how they 'feel' and how they look. They have peaceful vibes and often appear more angelic to me. Big meat eaters and dairy consumers often look unhealthy and a bit crazy to me and often have what I see as suffering and a kind of madness inside them. This might sound a bit harsh, but if you dont believe me, try it for yourself.

A really good friend of mine, Jack, when I first met him he was eating lots of meat and loved it, and thought vegans were pathetic and full of it. After getting to know him we had many conversations about life, love and death and once he heard my perspective on veganism he decided to try it out for himself. He is now one of the most committed vegans I know – and I can tell you honestly that his appearance and energy has changed quite radically. People who eat meat often look either pale, or bright red and often have a kind of white fatty look about them. Vegetarians and vegans develop a kind of golden look and their skin if often healthy and soft looking. Jack is now a golden vegan with peaceful vibes, im very proud of him.

These are all my own personal feelings surrounding this issue, and just how I feel from my heart, I know for some the meat eating thing can be a sensitive issue, but we all feel differently about these things and this is how I feel. In other cultures and countries at least they have a sacred, loving and respectful relationship with the animals that they rear and use for food and clothing. Often in some remote tribes in Mongolia for example they say a prayer and thank the gods and the animal before killing it and they also utilize every part of that animal. In the west animals are treated like a commodity, there is little to no honor and respect for the living soul that is present in the body of that being, and in my opinion treating a soul this way is an insult to god, the universe and ones own self because we too are souls, and to treat a soul without decency and respect is the same as insulting your own soul. There is also a wasteful attitude, and a lack of awareness for the fact that the meat that is being eaten came at the cost of another beings life. I cant count how many half-eaten burgers iv seen lying on the floor in the street or in the bin. This culture I feel is very out of touch with anything resembling what might be considered sacred and needs to grow and change.

Im not beating around the bush with this message because *I believe* if you eat meat I will be doing you a favor by making you more aware of the cycles of life you are getting involved in. You will have better karma if you genuinely live more peacefully and try to be mindful about the suffering that you cause. Eating meat produced by modern-day western farming methods often instantly links you to immense suffering because of the way it is done. I believe that it is important to adopt an attitude of non-violence towards nature. So, whenever possible, be non-violent towards animals, plants, insects and all life. 'Live, love, honour and let live'

A few - Tasty Vegan recipes –

Vegetable curry -
Ingredients:
440g/1lb sweet potatoes, chopped
2 tbsp sunflower oil
1 onion, chopped
1 red pepper, chopped
440g/1lb peas
225g/8oz green beans
1 tsp cumin seeds
1 tsp fennel seeds
1 tsp mustard seeds
1 tsp turmeric powder
2 cloves of garlic
½-1 tsp chilli powder, according to taste
1 can coconut milk
1 can of chopped tomatoes
1 can of chickpeas
2 tsp tomato puree
1 tsp veg stock (add to taste)
Method:
1. add all veg to pan and fry with seeds and spices.
2. add can of coconut milk and tomatoes and tomato puree and chickpeas
3. add veg stock and chilli and cook until veg is soft.

4. serve with boiled rice and garnish with fresh coriander and maybe side salad.

Vegetable risotto with creamy mushroom sauce

Ingredients:

2 cups of risotto rice
1 red pepper
2 white onion
1 courgette
10 cherry tomatoes
440g peas
Veg stock
Italian herbs
White wine
Soy cream
4 cloves of garlic
10 chestnut mushrooms
10 sticks of asparagus

Method:

1. chop all veg except one onion and 2 cloves of garlic.
2. add chopped veg to pan and fry lightly.
3. add 700ml of boiling water to the pan with the frying veg.
4. add risotto rice and veg stock to water and veg.
5. in a separate pan, chop and fry remaining onion and garlic and chestnut mushrooms.

6. add soy cream to mushroom pan. And 1tsp veg stock plus some Italian herbs.
7. add white wine to mushroom sauce.
8. lightly fry asparagus
9. serve veg risotto
10. pour over mushroom sauce
11. place fried asparagus on top.

Home-made hummus:
Ingredients:
1 large can of chickpeas
Juice from 1 lemon
2 tbsp Tahini
1 small clove of garlic
1 tsp sea salt
Sesame seeds

Method:
1. place all ingredients into a food processor or a bowl
2. blend either using the processor or with a hand blender in the bowl
3. sprinkle with sesame seeds and serve

Home-made walnut and red pepper pate
Ingredients:
1 large can of chickpeas
1 handful of walnuts

Juice from one lemon
1 small clove of garlic
1 red pepper
1 handful of chopped fresh parsley
2 tbsp Cajun seasoning (or mixed seasoning)
Half of a small red onion

Method:
1. place all ingredients into a bowl or a food processor
2. blend either using a hand blender or the processor
3. serve with maybe a sprinkle of paprika

FLOWER POWER

To further harmonize and be more at one with nature it can be a good idea to start trying to use alternatives to pharmaceutical and man-made products for health and well-being. Use natural soaps and beauty products. Indian Ayurvedic beauty products are often pretty good and contain natural ingredients. Also, if you use perfume, try using essential oils instead of synthetic products – I often use Lavender and/or Patchouli oil on my clothes, I just apply a few drops neat to my coat or shirt (can create oil blob stains so apply in dark area of clothes) and its great! I always get people telling me how nice I smell. Essential oils create a natural, soothing fragrance and are a million times nicer and cheaper then their synthetic alternatives. Try also to use natural toothpaste, washing powder, washing up liquid and any other products that are likely to contain strange chemicals. Nature knows best.

It is also a good idea to learn a few basic things from nature that you can use to help heal you and help improve your health. Nature has a lot of powerful remedies for you that can heal and harmonize the energies in your body. Here are just a few useful things from nature that you can use for everyday health.

Turmeric – Helps detox and purify the liver
Garlic – Powerful natural antibiotic – consume raw
Cloves – Powerful natural anesthetic – good for toothache
Ginger – Settles the stomach – eases nausea
Holy Basil – ease anxiety

Calendula – relieve inflammation and skin irritation
Echinacea - Antiviral and immune-enhancing properties
Ginseng - Helps relieve mental and physical fatigue
Licorice - For sore throats and coughs
Milk Thistle - Protects the liver
Valerian – Good for sleep

If your diet is full of raw fruits and vegetables you will be getting lots of lovely living enzymes, vitamins and minerals that will keep you healthy. Try and eat organic whenever possible to make an effort to avoid pesticides and chemicals used in food production. If you feel inclined growing your own food is a wonderful way to nourish your mind and body. Try to eat some good alkalizing foods that will help to remove excess acidity from your body – lots of leafy greens is a good idea for this and lemon also has an alkalizing effect. Good clean water is also essential, maybe try and source your water from a known and trusted spring or filter your water. Blessing your water and cultivating a loving relationship towards water will also help to harmonize your body.

Here is a quick nutrition reference guide for you to source key nutrients in your diet -
if you are sensible and eat plenty of fruits, vegetables, nuts, beans etc. you will be just fine. But to be sure, its always

handy to have something to refer too, especially if you are dealing with specific health issues.

Calcium

broccoli, green leafy vegetables (such as kale, bok choy, collard and turnip greens), tofu, blackstrap molasses, chickpeas, many beans, sesame seeds, sunflower seeds, almonds, flax seeds, brazil nuts, dried figs, dried fruit.

Iron

green leafy vegetables & sea vegetables, legumes/beans, nuts & seeds, blackstrap molasses, dried fruits, watermelon, prune juice, spinach, cereals, whole grains.

Magnesium

brown rice, cooked spinach, beans/legumes, almonds/nuts, dried figs, broccoli, cooked oatmeal, wheat germ/bran, whole grains, green leafy vegetables, bananas, peanuts.

Phosphorus

pinto beans, cereal grains, almonds, nuts, dried beans, peas, lentils, peanuts, brown rice, avocados, spinach, many vegetables, yeast.

Potassium

raisins, bananas, raw and cooked spinach, potatoes, baked sweet potatoes, winter squash, raw cauliflower, avocados, kiwifruit, dried fruits, tomatoes, oranges, grapefruit, strawberries, honeydew melon, cantaloupe, dried apricots.

Zinc

pumpkin seeds, whole grains/cereals, legumes, lentils, peas, soy foods, nuts, sunflower seeds, wheat germ, yeast, garbanzo beans, raw collard greens, spinach, corn.

Selenium

brazil nuts, whole grains, kidney beans (depending on the soil they are grown in), yeast.

Manganese

brown rice & whole grains, cereals, cooked oatmeal, wheat germ, nuts, seeds, legumes, cooked spinach & kale, black beans, almonds, avocados, pineapples, strawberries.

Pantothenic Acid

whole grain cereals, legumes, mushrooms, peanuts, soybeans, avocados, sunflower seeds, bananas, oranges, cooked collard greens, baked potato, broccoli.

Chromium

whole grains, nuts, broccoli, apples, peanuts, cooked spinach, mushrooms.

Biotin

cereals & whole grains, breads, yeast, almonds, peanuts, molasses, legumes.

Copper

nuts and seeds, whole grains, dried beans, mushrooms.

Folic Acid

legumes, lentils, oranges, whole grains, asparagus, spinach, romaine lettuce.

Iodine

iodine-rich sea vegetables, kelp, vegetables grown in iodine-rich soil.

Protein

Beans, lentils, nuts, seeds, many vegetables including broccoli, tofu, soy.

Vitamin A

carrots, winter squashes (acorn and butternut), sweet potatoes, cantaloupe, apricots, spinach, kale, turnip greens, broccoli, red bell peppers and other greens.

Vitamin B1 (Thiamin)

brown rice & whole grains, bread, pasta, oatmeal, brewers and nutritional yeast, legumes, cereals, sunflower seeds, nuts, watermelon, raw wheat germ.

Riboflavin

yeast, beans, cereals, whole grains, spinach, broccoli, wheat germ, mushrooms.

Vitamin B3 (Niacin)

legumes, brown rice, green vegetables, potatoes, tomatoes, broccoli.

Vitamin B6

whole grains, peanuts, nuts/legumes, soybeans, walnuts, bananas, watermelon

Vitamin C

bell peppers, broccoli, tomatoes, strawberries, oranges/orange juice, grapefruit, tomatoes, brussel sprouts, cabbage, collard greens, turnip greens, spinach, potatoes, melon, berries, papayas, romaine lettuce, watercress.

Vitamin D

The most significant supply of Vitamin D comes from sunlight exposure on the skin. Vitamin D-2 supplements are available, as well as Vitamin D fortified plant milks & cereals.

Vitamin E

vegetable oils, sunflower seeds, raw wheat germ, nuts, peanuts, green leafy vegetables, whole wheat flour, whole grains, spinach.

Vitamin K

green leafy vegetables, spinach, turnip greens, kale, parsley, brussel sprouts, broccoli, cauliflower, soybeans and soybean oil, cabbage, green tea, tomatoes.

Vitamin B12

Nutritional Yeast, B-12 fortified non-dairy milks and cereals. Vegan B-12 supplements, fermented soy products and spirullina has a compound similar to b12.

It is nice to develop a love and respect for nature to and to try and be gentle and loving to mother earth, taking only what you need and trying to replenish, nourish and help nature to flourish. Living in symbiosis means to live in a way which is mutually beneficial, a way that benefits all parties. It is the most sensible, sane and harmonious way to operate and most of the animal kingdom seem to live this way. Personally I try to tread lightly on the earth and try to be gentle. For instance, most people think that picking flowers is a nice thing to do, but if someone gives me flowers I feel sorry for them, i'd rather see the flowers alive, in the garden, vibrant, enjoying the sunshine and feeding the bees, I don't find them slowly dying in a vase a pleasing sight. Perhaps as an alternative to flowers, giving people a piece of fruit (which wants to be picked and eaten) would be a nice gesture instead? It makes me feel peaceful when I cultivate a gentleness, love and respect towards nature and to try and treat it as though it is sacred and divine, as though the whole world of nature is a holy temple.

HAIRY HIPPIES

Letting nature take it's course has long been part of the hippie way, and often this means letting your body do what it wants to do without to much interference from the mind and our perceptions. Hippie's are known for having hairy armpits, beards, long hair, hairy legs and hairy everything. Could there be a deeper reason for this choice to be hairy or is it just a fashion statement? Well, the more that I have investigated this the more iv discovered that there is far more to this question then I first realised.

According to Yogic scientific understanding, hair can actually help raise the Kundalini energy which helps to boost vitality, intuition, and calm. In times gone by people never thought about cutting their hair because it was part of who they were and was considered to be a source of power. In the past people used to cut the hair of prisoners as a punishment to take away their power, take for instance the story of Samson from the Bible who lost his power when his almighty dreadlocks were cut off. The science of hair was explained by Yogi Bhajan when he first came to America.

He believed that when hair on our head is allowed to attain its full length, phosphorous, calcium, and vitamin D are all produced at a greater level of efficiency. The nutrients then enter the lymphatic fluid, and eventually the spinal fluid through two ducts on the top of the brain. This results in a more efficient memory and leads to greater physical energy, improved stamina, and patience."

Yogi Bhajan believed that if you choose to cut your hair, you lose this boost of energy and nourishment and your body must then provide vital energy and nutrients to continually re-grow the missing hair.

In addition, hairs are also thought to be antennas that

receive and transmit cosmic sun energy (a.k.a. prana) to our frontal lobes (part of the brain we use for meditation and visual imagination). These magic antennas act as conduits to bring us increased amounts of subtle, cosmic light energy. It is thought to take up to three years from the last time your hair was cut for new antennas to form at the tips of the hair.

In India, a Rishi is considered to be a wise one who winds his or her hair up on the top of the head during daylight to energize the brain cells, and then unwinds and combs it down at night. A 'rishi knot' is believed to energize the bodies magnetic field (aura) and stimulate the pineal gland in the center of your brain. The Pineal glad is also known as the 'Third eye' and is considered to be our cosmic link to the metaphysical universe. René Descartes believed the pineal gland to be the "principal seat of the soul" and conspiracy theorists around the world believe that those who are attempting to control the 'masses' have directly targeted this glad to disable some of our more important powers (such as telepathy and e.s.p) by adding flouride to the water and aspartame to our food (two toxic substances found to directly cause damage to the pineal glad.)

Yogi Bhajan believed that the activation of the Pineal gland results in a secretion that is central to the development of higher intellectual functioning, as well as higher spiritual perception.

During the daytime, the hair absorbs cosmic solar energy, but at night it absorbs lunar energy. Keeping the hair up during the day and down at night is thought to improve the efficiency of this process. Braiding your hair at night is also thought to help the bodies electromagnetic field (aura) balance out from the day.

If you think about our culture and our fashion trends we see that 'skin heads' and people who shave off all of their hair are often seen as insensitive and aggressive people whereas people with long hair are often seen as peace loving hippies. Women traditionally have long hair and are thought to be more sensitive and in touch with nature and their emotions then men who commonly have short hair. If a man chooses to grow his hair long it is common for him to be considered to be effeminate and sensitive and perhaps more in touch with his emotions. Perhaps there is a real reason for these perceptions and hair does actually have a purpose and a function for our bodies and our awareness. Some consider hair to be a direct extension to our nervous systems and a link which helps us to sensitize us to more subtle energies around us. Many animals are very in touch with their hairs and for some they play a vital part in their sensory perceptions i.e. Cat's whiskers.

Yogi Bhajan's top tips for hair care

If you have split ends apply some almond oil and leave it overnight. Then during the day keep the hair coiled and protected allowing time for the hair to heal. Be very gentle with the hair and use natural soaps and oils, and avoid using blow dryers and any harsh chemicals on the hair.

Wash the hair every 72 hours with natural soaps and if you have had a period of difficult emotions it is thought that washing your hair will help to clear any difficult energies from your body. It is also recommended that you use a wooden comb when brushing your hair as it will help circulation and stimulate the scalp without producing static electricity which can interfere with the hairs energy that it sends to the brain. Regular combing will help to reduce tiredness and if you comb the hair twice a day it has been found to improve eyesight, maintain a youthful appearance and help regulate the menstrual cycle for women.

If you are starting to loose your hair naturally the lack of hair energy can be counteracted by doing more meditation. If your hair is starting to turn silver this can actually be a good thing as its the bodies natural way to increase energy flow and vitamins to the brain to help counteract the process of aging. The silver and white colour improves the hair's ability to transmit energy and vitamins.

Yogi Bhajan states that "Your hair is not there by mistake. It has a definite purpose, which saints will discover and other men will laugh at."

ART

Being creative is an important part of discovering oneself and is a common practice of many hippies... but what is art and why do we do it?

I believe art is a projection of mind. It is a form that has arisen from a thought. It is an attempt to explore the self. To project into the world something deep from within the mind so it can be experienced, observed and interacted with. Art is an attempt to look into the mirror. It is a bridge that is built between the inner and outer world. It is a symbol that represents an intangible experience of consciousness. Art is an energetic imprint that is left on the world which represents the journey the artist made through consciousness. When I share my creativity with people I am attempting to reach out and connect. It is a way of expressing A depth of being that is impossible to define. Art is the voice of dreams and imagination. It is a language spoken by all. Art uses the facets of reality for its incarnation. It deals with colour, sound, the elements- these ancient and sacred modes of reality that are the voices of eternity, of the divine.

Art seems to me to also be an expression of universal truth and the collective consciousness that is shared by all. Creativity is a method of connecting with the universe and to merge with it. As I create, my creations affect the course of my reality until I end up living in a world that is shaped by my dreams and projections. Creativity and art it is a direct reminder and illustration of how mind and reality interact. It can dissolve the borders between the world outside the head and the world inside the head- bringing the two worlds together. Art can also be an offering to what I call the divine. The process of devotion, concentration, mindfulness and focus that Is applied when taking the time to create is about honoring life and giving a gift to the divine. It is a spiritual practice that leads to the exploration of the world within.

Art has the capacity to unite people. If something is communicated through art that represents a universal truth often many people resonate with it and can feel what it represents. Art can enliven the spirit and inspire action in people.

Art can be an echo from the soul, from touching the void we can bring back symbols, paintings, expressions to show what we have seen, what we have felt. Art has the power to communicate messages that can change consciousness on an individual and even global level. Use your creative skills to shine your truth, your love, your joy – in the hope that it may awaken the sleeping Buddha within our hearts. Let the rays of light shine out from the soul and warm our hearts and minds like gentle rays from the ever-loving sun. like an inquisitive ear the mind and soul listens, in the hope of discovering the holy grail, so that it may rest in eternity. Art can help guide us home, can help to create signposts and show us the way. Art can speak of that which cannot be spoken and attempt to express the inexpressible. Om Shanti.

ONE SENTENCE THOUGHTS

A wise man is a happy man.
When I breathe out the world breathes in.
See yourself in everything.
The pathway of peace is always there for those who wish to walk it.
Life cannot live without death.
Spirituality is simple honesty.
My god is everything and my religion is love.
All we can know is what we are.
There is no destination, only a journey.
Why not now? Tomorrow never comes.
Is there anything more mind blowing than the mind itself?
How big is eternity?
Everything is speaking we just need to listen.
We are both the teacher and the student.
Formless is the womb out of which form is born.
Nothing is ever lost or found, it just is.
Present a key that fits.
Old people remind me of clouds.
Time is not money, the money is time.
Nothing is unnatural.
Whatever happened is the only thing that could have happened.

All things are subjective when filtered through the senses.
Objectivity is letting go.
Evidence is everywhere proof is nowhere.
No proof means no knowing.
No knowing accepts all possibilities.
There is no space in between only seamless connection.
Space represents perceptual limitation.
There is no end; there is no beginning, to my sense of being.
If death is a cessation of being, death cannot be experienced; therefore death doesn't exist for the individual.
There is only life for the individual.
Life cannot live without death.
Love is realising harmony.
Love brings a sense of connection and unity.
Time is the speed of perception.
Time is a four letter word.
Now never stays still.
Dreams are timeless.
Can anything ever be added that is not already there?
Love is the force that gives life. Love is life-force.
Silence is Loud.
Love is peace.
Peace is truth.
Life is a living poem.

Truth when spoken is heard by all.
Everything has equal value.
All we have is what we are.
Existence is the only thing we have.
Because we all only have existence, we are all equal.
We are all in the same boat.
The only thing we can know is reality itself.
Science matters not to a rainbow.
Theories cannot change realities on a fundamental level.
The format for reality is a set playing field.
All possibility is known and contained within the fabric of eternity.
Eternity knows no limits.

PEACE

POEMS

Love is the glue that binds you to me
The leaves to the trees
The moon to the sea
You have to believe if you want to be free
Love is the force of eternity

Beyond white wheels and shifting tides a sphere of eyes glistens.
Ruby red and emerald green are noticed by the not to be seen as a presence neither man nor machine, listens.
Form and figure take many shapes and no conclusions are made.
Ideas flashing curiously with colour are embraced and forgotten in this ever weaving wind of symmetrical difference like a peacock's plumage in a playful parade.

I am a willpower that seems to persist.
I am a watcher that feels it exists.
I am a moment that can think and sense.
I am not knowing if I am here by chance.

I am beauty, I'm all around
In the air, in the ground
the crashing waves of the sea
In dreams that spring endlessly
The sun, the moon, the whole of space
In every time and every place
I sit and wait to be revealed
For peaceful minds who see the real.

The forest, the tree, a water wave
The boundless sea, a crystal cave
An island beyond, the earth below
Combined and united by a simple glow-

The feeling I get.
The feeling I get as my world unfolds
Like petals of light on an etheric rose
The essence stays as my body grows
To a destination no-one knows.

A seemingly seamless expressionist whole
Both inner and outer, yet nothing at all
Its all for one and one for all
Nothing is set- Its a feeling I get.

Recommended hippie reading list

Cosmic Trigger – Robert Anton Wilson
Doors of perception – Aldous Huxley
The Way it is – Ajahn Sumedho
The Tao Te Ching – Lao Tsu
Yoga Sutra's - Patanjali
The secrets of water – Dr masuro emoto
Who am I? - The teaching of Sri Ramana Maharishi

ST FRANCIS OF ASSISI SACRED PRAYER

Lord, make me an instrument of Your peace. Where there is hatred, let me sow love; where there is injury, pardon; where there is doubt, faith; where there is despair, hope; where there is darkness, light; where there is sadness, joy.

O, Divine Master, grant that I may not so much seek to be consoled as to console; to be understood as to understand; to be loved as to love; For it is in giving that we receive; it is in pardoning that we are pardoned; it is in dying that we are born again to eternal life.

Printed in Poland
by Amazon Fulfillment
Poland Sp. z o.o., Wrocław

56175468R00060